A NEW LOOK AT
FELT

Appliqué,
Stitchery,
and Sculpture

by Elyse and Mike Sommer

CROWN PUBLISHERS, INC., NEW YORK

Acknowledgments

In the course of gathering material for this book we encountered artists in all parts of the world who are doing outstanding work. It is their generosity in sharing their work with us that made it possible to give proof that felt can indeed be used as a serious art fabric as well as an easy, fun medium. A very special bravo goes to Barbara Setsu Pickett who permitted us an exciting preview of her still-developing experiments in the new-old art of making felt.

Our thanks to Andy, Lorna, Lucy, and Peggy for their modeling services; to Alan and Ben Ageman for processing our pictures with their usual skill, promptness, and good cheer.

ELYSE and MIKE SOMMER
Woodmere, L.I., N.Y., 1975

All illustrated work, unless otherwise identified, by Elyse Sommer.
All photographs, unless otherwise identified, by Mike Sommer.

© *1975 by Elyse Sommer*
All rights reserved. No part of this book may be reproduced or utilized in any form or by any means, electronic or mechanical, including photocopying, recording, or by any information storage or retrieval system, without permission in writing from the publisher.
Inquiries should be addressed to Crown Publishers, Inc.,
419 Park Avenue South, New York, N.Y. 10016.
Printed in the United States of America
Published simultaneously in Canada by
General Publishing Company Limited

Designed by Ruth Smerechniak and Margaret C. Lewis

Library of Congress Cataloging in Publication Data

Sommer, Elyse.
   A new look at felt.

   Bibliography: p.
   Includes index.
   1. Felt work.   I.   Sommer, Mike, joint author.
II.   Title.
TT880.S664   1975   746'.04'63   75-11794
ISBN 0-517-51860-0
ISBN 0-517-51861-9 pbk.

Contents

Felt appliqué on wool by Kopel Gurwin. Photographed at the Israeli Art Center.

Foreword

According to legend, Noah covered the floor of the ark with wool plucked from the backs of sheep in order to make the voyage more comfortable. When the animals left the ark, Noah discovered that they had trampled and moistened the loose wool into a compacted fabric. This, if the legend is to be believed, is how felt was produced for the first time.

Textile historians attribute the use and discovery of feltmaking techniques to Mongol nomads of ancient Central Asia. Unlike more settled people who would use rigid materials for building their houses, they needed a material that was light and unbreakable and that could be transported from place to place. Since the nomads were a primitive people who kept no records, it is hard to pinpoint the discovery of the feltmaking process to an exact date of a specific tribe. However, historians feel certain that the Chinese, Tibetans, Indians, Iranians, Turks, and Russians, who did include frequent references to felt in their histories (some dating back as far as 2300 B.C.), learned to make and use felt from nomads as they wandered through their countries.

Since the nomads were considered uncivilized, felt was long thought of as a material of barbarians. Nevertheless the use of felt spread for both ceremonial and functional purposes. In China ceremonial felt mats were used for the emperor. Felt hats and tents were symbolic of rank. The Russian Cossacks used the material so widely that they were known by other troops as the Felt Army. The earliest felt remains now in existence are believed to be those unearthed by Sir Aurel Stein from ancient refuse heaps and buried temple ruins of Chinese Turkestan. These have been preserved in the British Museum.

The legend surrounding Noah's ark as the first felt factory, so to speak, is very popular among modern felt manufacturers because it so simply and vividly sums up the basic processes involved in feltmaking, whether by primitive hand methods or by modern machinery:

Raw fibers are treated to the shock of repeated pressure and moisture until the fibers are fulled or felted into a firm material. In the primitive handmade process, raw wool is spread out on a mat, layer upon layer, until the desired thickness is achieved; the wool is then moistened (sometimes with hot water, sometimes with grease mixed with water) and rolled up in a mat, with much kneading and pounding as it is rolled. The wool is rolled and rerolled from first one end and then the other, until the felting of fibers is effected.

1

Felt and the
Artist-Craftsman

Since felt is a nonwoven material, it can be cut without unraveling. Its ease of handling makes possible great spontaneity of design. The illustrations throughout this book best exemplify the range of possibilities for both easy and fun art as well as serious work.

While the availability of the wide spectrum of colors in commercial felt has added to the fabric's attraction as an art material, even the stark grays and blacks of industrial felts have served artists well.

Joseph Beuys, a German artist, has become world famous for his gray felt suits, made in limited editions and sold to serious collectors of modern art.

Mr. Beuys also gives performances such as his recent "I Love America—America Loves Me" show at the René Block Gallery in New York's SoHo. The artist appeared on stage in a portable felt "environment." While at least some of the audience may have been mystified by the artist's unusual felt environment and the presence of a live coyote, the effect was undeniably forceful.

Another artist attracted to industrial felt is Robert Morris. Although he has worked with many other industrial materials, Morris is particularly well known for his draped and shaped assemblages and hangings of heavy gray and black felt.

"Filanzug" (Felt Suit) by Joseph Beuys, numbered label edition of 100 published by René Block. Photo courtesy René Block Gallery.

Joseph Beuys' performance of "I Love America . . . America Loves Me." Courtesy René Block Gallery.

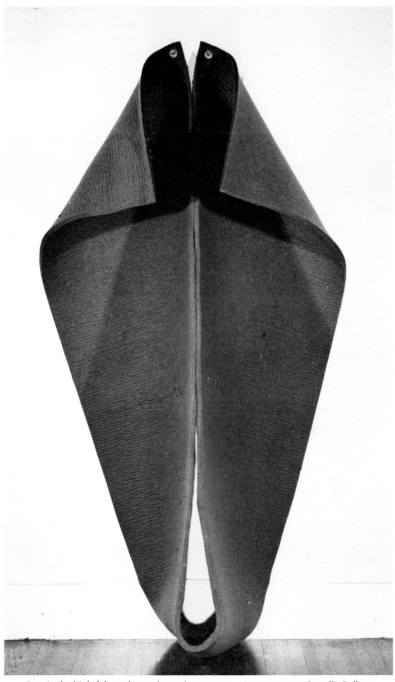

One-inch thick felt sculpture by Robert Morris. Courtesy Leo Castelli Gallery.

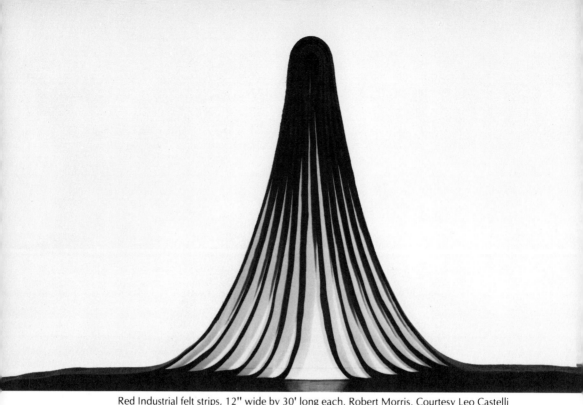

Red Industrial felt strips, 12" wide by 30' long each. Robert Morris. Courtesy Leo Castelli Gallery.

Modular banner of felt and vinyl. Roy Lichtenstein. Courtesy Leo Castelli Gallery.

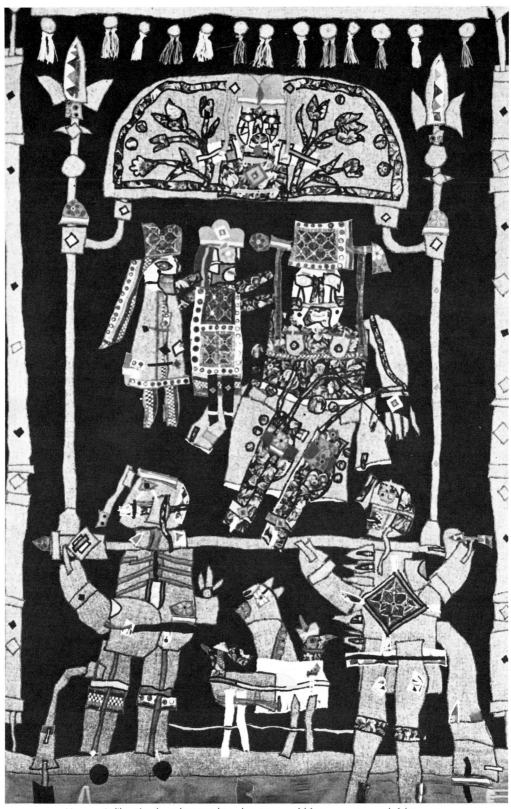

Norman Laliberté, whose banners have become world famous, uses much felt to express the pure love of life grown men and women search for and children possess. "Gloriana," 58" X 93", courtesy Arras Gallery.

Most of the artists we've interviewed work with commercially made felt, and for this reason the examples throughout this book are designed with commercial felt. However, our history of felt would be incomplete without some attention to a small but growing movement by textile scholars and artists to experiment with ancient methods of feltmaking. With the enormous revival of interest in old crafts, it seems almost incredible that one of the oldest man-made fabrics has been virtually ignored by those in the textile arts who have so enthusiastically embraced weaving and spinning. A few schools such as Cranbrook Academy in Michigan and California State University have done some work in this area.

The reader interested in experimentation can do a very simple and basic experiment in felting simply by carding or combing some raw fleece (see sources of supplies), arranging the fleece to fit the bottom of his shoes, and keeping the clumps of fleece in the shoes for a week or so. (This is the most comfortable experiment you're likely to make in your lifetime.) Different colors of fleece can be layered to make these footprints and the resultant small piece of art fabric will have a unique quality of its own. Primitive and uneven as it may be, it can nevertheless be cut with the edges remaining smooth, just like commercial felt.

Tina Johnson, a young Californian, agreed to do some larger experimental pieces especially for this book. Her process, while not quite as simple as the footprint fabric, can be carried out with ordinary methods and equipment. Her use of the washing machine and dryer is certainly something the old-time feltmakers might have appreciated.

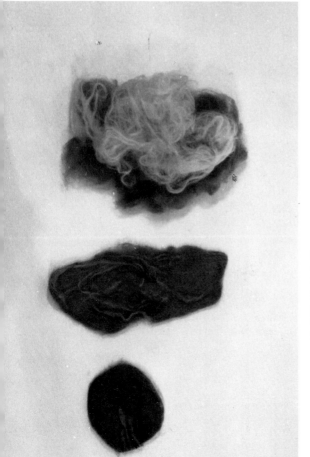

From top to bottom: Teased and carded fleece layered in preparation to placing inside shoe for felting: . . . . the felted footprint. . . . . . the footprint cut into a circular form, showing hard, smooth edges.

Layered Fleece Felted in Washing Machine–Dryer

Carded and teased fleece arranged in large layers.

Dark fleece added to the completed batt to add design.

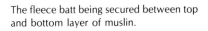

The fleece batt being secured between top and bottom layer of muslin.

After the muslin-encased fleece has been washed in hot water in machine, and dried in dryer, it is removed from the muslin case.

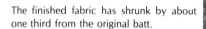

The finished fabric has shrunk by about one third from the original batt.

Tina fashioned her felt fabric into a hat, using knotless netting for finishing details. Photographer-model, Bob Zvolensky.

Barbara Setsu Pickett of Portland, Oregon, is experimenting with feltmaking on a somewhat more ambitious scale. She has just equipped a studio specifically to turn out large pieces of felt. In the following photo sequence she gives us a fascinating glimpse of her studio and her methods.

Barbara uses a carding machine to expedite the fleece-carding process.

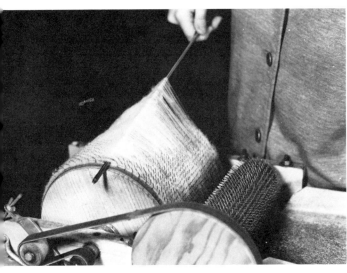

A rod is inserted into the fleece to remove the batt.

The fleece is arranged into batts. Here are two batts side by side.

Barbara applies her design to the top layer.

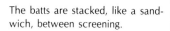

The batts are stacked, like a sandwich, between screening.

Hot water is poured over the batt.

The "sandwich" is placed on a drainboard and a soapy solution, which acts as a binding agent, is rubbed all over the surface.

The rinsed cloth is folded into a packet . . .

. . . and immersed in a bath of boiling water.

Barbara rolls the cloth on the drainboard . . .

and presses it in a mangle.

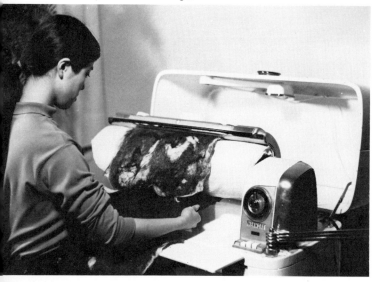

The finished cloth has a rich texture and unique coloring.

Basic Materials
and Methods

You'll need very few extras besides the felt itself, and most of those will more than likely be among your general household and needlework supplies. As for skills needed to work with felt—if you can cut, glue, sew, and stitch, you're ready to work.

Buying Felt

Felt is available in practically any store that sells fabrics. It comes in 39- and 72-inch widths (many stores carry only the 72-inch width) and also in precut squares and sometimes in mixed bags of colors and sizes. While the felt squares may seem cheap as compared to the cost per yard, it is usually more economical to buy your felt by the yard. You can buy as little as a third of a yard and you can always find some use for the leftovers, even if only to line a box or cover the bottom of something resting on a scratchable surface.

As you work with felt, *save every scrap.* The tiniest dot can be used as part of a banner, to trim a doll, to make a mosaic.

Most felts sold in fabric stores are made of wool mixed with other fibers such as rayon and are quite thin. The more wool content, the better the quality of your felt. As a rule, if you want felt containing 50 percent or more wool, you will have to buy it through decorators or order it from felt specialists (see sources of supplies). Actually, thin felts

Scraps of yellow and gold felt are machine-stitched into a handsome mosaic. Charlotte Patera. Courtesy artist.

Bits of many colors are stitched into a mosaic depicting the colors of "Earth and Sky." 27" X 21". Caroline Wickham. Courtesy artist.

have the advantage of being easily layered. If you are a machine sewer, you can sew through three or four layers of thin felt on the machine. As the felt is stacked it attains its own thickness and richness. The very heavy industrial type felts are in fact layers of felt laminated into one.

Tools and Equipment

You'll be doing a lot of cutting so good scissors are probably your most important tools when working with felt. You'll need large shears and embroidery scissors for cutting out small pieces and for sewing and stitching.

Since felt is a crisp fabric that cuts as smoothly as paper, we decided to try cutting it with a paper cutter, and this turned out to be an excellent cutting tool. The paper cutter is especially handy when cutting lots of small pieces, as for patchwork and for thin strips.

For accurate cutting it is best to mark felt. You will need a ruler, tailor's chalk for dark fabrics, and a pencil for light fabrics.

Very smooth crisp felt is easier to work with, so a steam iron should be kept at hand to use both before you start and after a project is completed. If you keep your felt pieces neatly folded in boxes or plastic bags, you'll have a minimum of beforehand ironing.

Felt can be either glued permanently or glue-basted. White glue is best suited for felt. When gluing temporarily, we suggest that you dilute the glue by ⅓ with water. For any kind of gluing, be sure to apply the adhesive to the surface to be covered rather than to the felt itself. This prevents saturating the material.

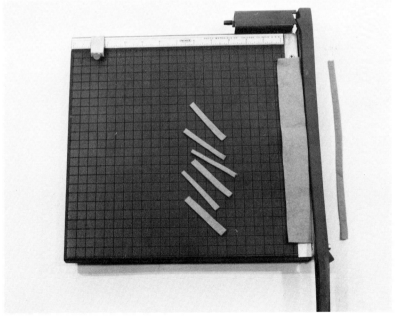

Felt can be cut on a paper cutter into strips as narrow as a quarter of an inch.

Australian artist Fay Bottrell does felt works on a large scale. Fabrics are stored at the far end of her studio to permit plenty of room for working. Courtesy artist.

MISCELLANEOUS ACCESSORIES:
Stuffing—old wool, cut-up pantyhose, Dacron, shredded foam. Beads, sequins, bits of lace and trims, buttons for contrasts, cotton, burlap hopsacking, or prints for contrasting backgrounds. Thumbtacks, staple guns, paper punches.

Sewing Felt

Sewing is probably the most popular way to laminate pieces of felt. Unlike other fabrics, felt can be sewn without seam allowances so that two pieces can be attached with a plain overhand sewing stitch, blanket stitch, or backstitch. Felt can be sewn by hand or sewing machine depending upon your preference. Many felt artists use a combination of hand and machine sewing.

Fay Bottrell uses a sewing machine for most of her
soft-hard-edge designs.

Machine stitching is very firm as seen in this close-up of one of Fay Bottrell's
hangings.

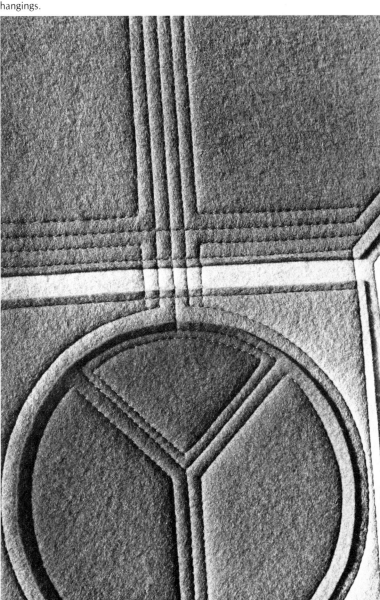

Decorative Sewing—Embroidery

Felt and embroidery are as compatible as apple pie and ice cream. You can make a lovely hanging by gluing felt to a background, without ever taking a needle in hand. However, if you look at Sharon Fields's jungle plaque before and after embroidery, you will see how much embroidery can enrich the basic felt shapes.

Felt designs on linen before the addition of stitchery. Sharon Fields.

Sharon added lots of hand stitchery and the results quite clearly speak for themselves. (See color section.)

Allover embroidery distinguishes this felt rug from India. Collection of the authors.

Basic Embroidery Skills

You do not need to be an experienced embroiderer to add stitchery to your felt designs. A running stitch, which is simply a small basting stitch, could see you through practically any project. You can vary the looks of the stitch by using different yarns. Some artists combine hand and machine embroidery.

Following are some of the most popular embroidery stitches:

THE RUNNING STITCH is a truly all-purpose stitch. Simply bring the needle in and out of the fabric. You can vary the stitch by varying your thread or yarn, the length of the stitch, or its direction.

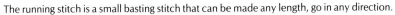

The running stitch is a small basting stitch that can be made any length, go in any direction.

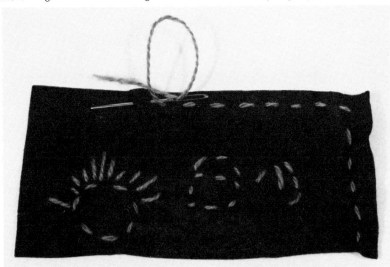

THE BACKSTITCH is usually thought of as a sewing stitch. Begin like a running stitch but bring the point of the needle back to the first stitch to fill in the space. Keep going forward and backward. The straight line may be varied by bringing your needle back just slightly above the middle of the last stitch.

The needle is brought back to the first stitch when making a backstitch. The straight line may be varied by bringing the needle back slightly above the middle of the last stitch.

SATIN STITCH. This is a filler stitch made by placing one straight stitch right next to another. Stitches can be vertical, horizontal or slanted.

Satin stitch.

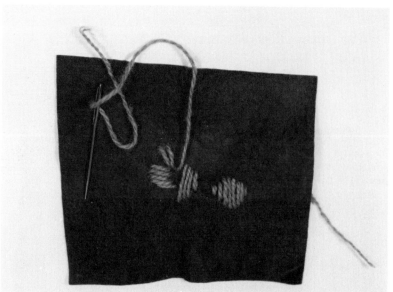

OVERHAND and BLANKET STITCHES are your most useful stitches for sewing down appliqués or attaching two pieces of felt at the edges. The overhand stitch is made by pushing the needle through the felt from back to front, either at an angle or straight up and down. The blanket stitch is a somewhat more decorative version. Start as you would for a straight overhand stitch but, before pulling the thread tight, weave the needle under the loop.

Overhand stitch, either slanted or straight up and down. Blanket stitch made by weaving needle underneath loop before pulling thread closed.

CROSS-STITCH. This is made by making one stitch at an angle and passing another across it. Cross-stitches can be made as individual crosses or as rows of crosses. By making one cross over another you can build a star design.

Cross-stitch.

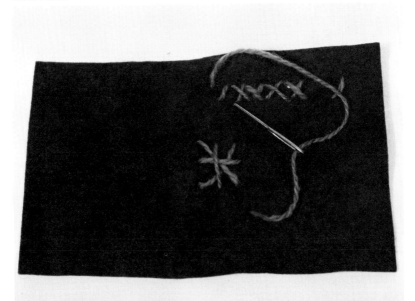

CHAIN STITCH is a great favorite with embroiderers. Bring the needle up from the back of the fabric. Make a loop and hold it down with your thumb. Bring your needle out and under the loop thread. Variations can be created by leaving the top of the loop open.

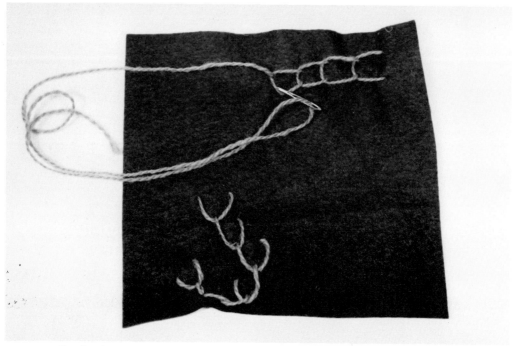

Closed and open chain stitch.

FRENCH KNOTS are great accent stitches. Knots in different colors and yarns can suggest a whole garden of flowers. Bring the thread up to the top of the fabric. Wind the thread around the needle three times and insert the needle down through the fabric, right next to where the thread came up.

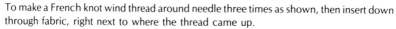

To make a French knot wind thread around needle three times as shown, then insert down through fabric, right next to where the thread came up.

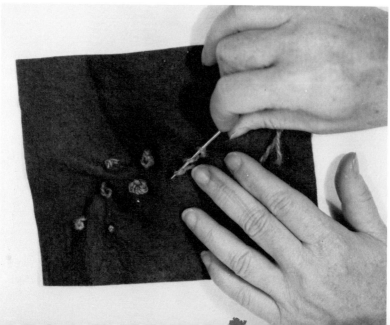

COUCHING is not really a stitch but a method of tacking down heavy yarn or a number of yarn strands, using a simple overhand stitch or just about any embroidery stitch.

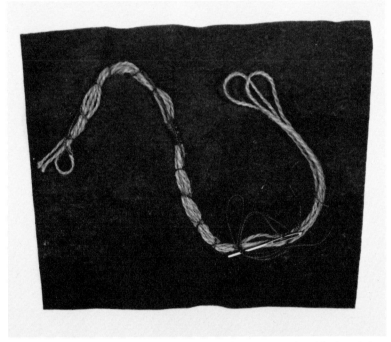

Heavy yarns can be couched with overhand stitches, cross-stitches, blanket stitches.

The Care and Maintenance of Felt

Few things are perfect and felt too has its drawbacks, the foremost of these being its tendency to fade when exposed to the rays of the sun. Few houses, apartments, or offices are bright enough throughout to make this fact a deterrent to using decorative felt pieces. It is more than likely that you will want a bright felt piece to lighten a dark area. Anyone overly concerned about the fading factor can of course stick to the less colorful neutrals and avoid those colors that tend to fade most easily, namely purples and blues.

Felt can be cleaned. We've cleaned felt clothing, pillows, and small hangings in the coin machines. While some people wash things made from felt in mild soap and cool water, we prefer to treat any handmade item as something special and apart from the weekly wash. We did have occasion to wash a lot of felt involuntarily when the waste from our dishwasher burst recently and caused a flood in our basement where the felt was stored. We were so sure that the felt was completely ruined that we used pieces of it to mop up some of the water (it proved highly absorbent and thus very efficient for this purpose). Later we decided

Marilyn Motz uses wool couching to create an appliqué design and border for a handsome tunic.

that since the felt was ruined anyway we might as well experiment with machine washing and drying our flood-soaked material. We used hot water and heat, and surprisingly the felt neither ran nor shrank. The washed and dried fabric lacked the crisp smoothness associated with felt, but it had a texture of its own which we found quite interesting. Thus, while this experiment would not alter our advice about washing and drying things made with new felt, it might indeed be something to do before you begin working if you want a fabric that does not have a typical felt look. Before long, nylon felts are likely to be generally available. These will require even fewer precautions in respect to light exposure and cleaning.

To protect felt from dirt and thus keep the whole question of cleaning within the now-and-then realm, you can treat everything you make with several spray applications of a fabric protector like Scotchgard. Be sure to use any spray out of doors and keep abreast of reports about any chemicals and their effect on the environment or you. Felt items for any sort of heavy-duty utility can be encased in plastic. (See some of the designs by Joan Schulze.)

3

Appliqué

The name *appliqué* is a French word which in turn is derived from the Latin word *applicare*, meaning to join or attach. Applied, or "laid on," work has a long history. Applied lacework has been practiced from the thirteenth century in India and Persia, where it was probably invented. In Italy, Germany, France, and England, it became identified not only with lace but referred to any type of textile material sewn to another.

Felt lends itself particularly well to appliqué since it requires no notching and tucking under of edges. Any shape or form can be cut out spontaneously and applied to a background of felt or other material. Felt appliqués can be glued or sewn. Some artists glue-baste their appliqués, using just a dot of glue to hold the felt to the background, then stitching down the edges. Felt can be heat-bonded by cutting out any of the commercially treated bonding fabrics to match the appliqué and then steam-pressing the appliqué to the backgrounds. These bonding materials can also be used in lieu of pinning or basting.

When sewing appliqués, a small running stitch is fast and very attractive on felt. Overhand stitches and blanket stitches can also be used. If you have a zigzag machine, it can be used to good advantage to zigzag or satin-stitch your appliqués. However, this is not something to do just for the sake of speed. A nicely satin-stitched appliqué takes some skill to execute and mistakes are time-consuming and difficult to undo. Thus machine appliqué is advisable for the look it gives more than as a time-saver.

Types of Appliqué Designs

Leaves, hearts, circles, triangles, trees, figures—in short, practically any form can be cut out of felt to make the basis for an appliqué design. You can cut your shapes free-form or draw them onto the fabric (pencil for light fabrics, tailor's chalk for dark fabric). One of the easiest ways to get started in felt appliqué is to use the paper folding and cutting methods you undoubtedly learned back in kindergarten. You can make your folds and cuts directly into the felt. If you use more than one fold, it is important to keep your design very simple. The thinnest felt sold is recommended.

Folded Petal Appliqué

A square of felt is folded in half, and in half again.

A third fold is made, the fat triangle is pinned and two arcs are marked off with tailor's chalk. It is best to cut the inside arc first. As each arc is cut the petal unfolds.

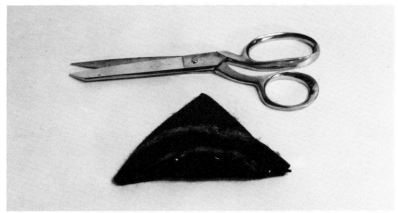

Here's what can be done with your petal appliqué designs. A large petal is used as the center motif for a pillow top. Smaller petals have one corner cut off and are placed all around the pillow. The pillow top is made in a layer of yellow, a smaller layer of black, a second layer of yellow, plus the appliqué, giving it all a rich quilted look. The pillow top and back are sewn together on three sides with the right sides facing in. The pillow is turned inside out and stuffed, then sewn together on the fourth side. The inside-out sewing method results in nicely rounded corners.

Felt Snowflakes

Snowflake designs allow for more intricate cutting since they are based on a single fold. This is the method employed for the much-coveted Hawaiian quilts. There are so many possibilities for designs that it's best to make lots of paper samples first and then select the designs you like best to work out in felt.

Lots of 4-inch squares of paper were folded in half and practice designs were drawn and cut. The ones to be used were then refolded and pinned to folded felt squares.

Small pointed scissors are needed for this type of cutting. Make your inside cuts first. Use the tip of the scissors to get started and cut with the shank of the scissors as you go around intricate curves.

Six of the snowflakes are appliquéd to a felt body or wall hanging. The bottom half can be unbuttoned to make the necklace waist length. The buttons are tiny, stuffed felt pillows.

The collar buttons onto a neckband with a casing at the top. The casing can accommodate a piece of driftwood or a dowel so that it can be used as a wall hanging when not in use.

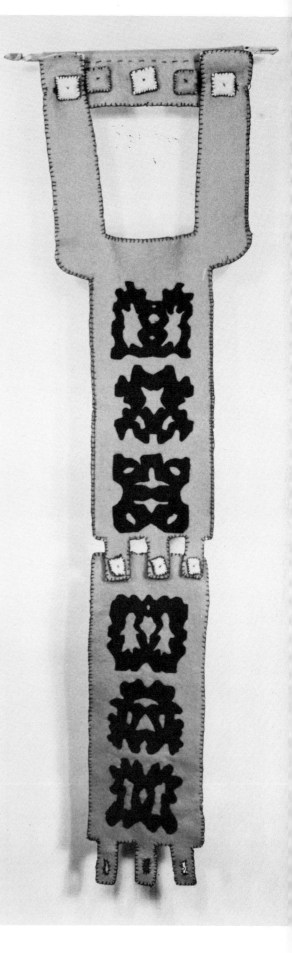

Reverse Appliqué

The method of making appliqués by cutting through layers of colored cloth and exposing the various layers underneath was perfected by the women of the San Blas Islands off the coast of Panama. The traditional cut-through appliqués, or molas, have become collectors' items and are difficult and complicated to make.

Reverse appliqué can be greatly simplified when working with felt since there is no need to notch and sew down cut edges. Let's see how this works with a small 4-layered felt mola design. On page 92 you will see how the finished mola, which measures just 8 inches square, was worked into a large convertible wall hanging–body ornament.

"Mola" from the collection of Gretchen Andersen.

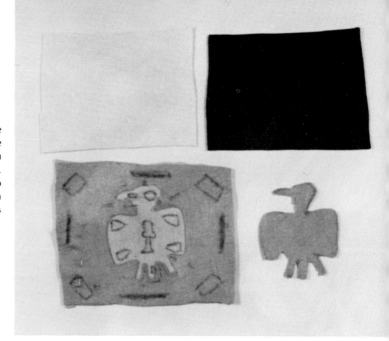

The sample mola is made with four layers of felt. The main motif was drawn on the top layer and cut out. The cut top is then pinned to the second layer, and both are marked for further cuts to be made.

Here is the design with cuts made into the first, second, and third layers, and a fourth placed underneath. Everything is pinned and ready to be sewn.

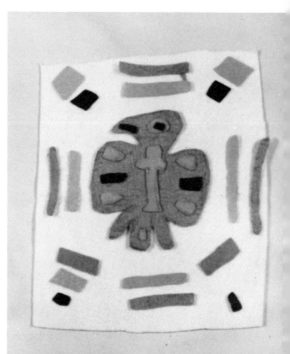

Don't throw away the cutout portions, but glue-baste them on another felt square to form an appliqué wall hanging.

Applied and Reverse Appliqué Ornaments

Ornaments that could double as pendants can be made by cutting out a basic shape in three different colors of felt. A cutting outline is drawn half to three-quarters of an inch from the edge of the piece that is to be the top layer. After the outlined shape is cut out of the top layer, the second layer is pinned to the top one (this is actually a frame) and another half to three-quarters of an inch is marked off and cut away, using the *inside* edge as a guide. The same procedure is followed for the bottom layer. The ornament is then turned over and the cutaway sections from the front are pinned to the back, in graduated size order. A bit of stuffing can be worked in between some of these applied layers. Running stitches are then made through all the layers.

Applied and reverse appliqué ornaments. The center hexagon shows the reverse appliqué technique. The two end shapes have the applied appliqué sides facing out.

Useful Felt Appliqué Projects

APPLIQUÉD HANDBAG

When making a bag in felt, the body and the handle can be cut all in one piece. To give the bag strength, it is advisable to use a top layer of felt, a lining layer of felt *plus* an in-between layer of interfacing or other stiff fabric. Handles can be lightly stuffed for softness and body. Decorative appliqués can be sewn just to the top layer of fabric or through top-interfacing-lining layers.

The appliqués are over-stitched to the front and back sides of the handbag, which is cut all in one piece. Extra layers of felt are cut in a contrasting shade to be used as a lining. See the right-hand portion of the photo. Sandwiched in between is a layer of interfacing.

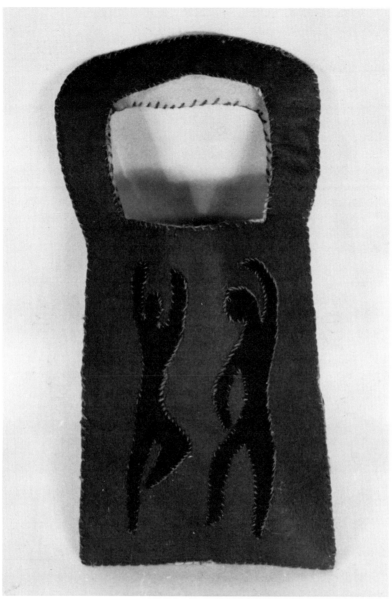

The finished handbag.

REVERSE APPLIQUÉ BELT

This belt is made of two layers of felt, one light and one dark. Circles and diamonds are cut out of the light felt so that the darker color shows through. Small running stitches outline the cut-through designs and the belt edge. The buckle is cut from a double layer of felt, with some stuffing and lightweight wire sewn in between.

The principle of placing cutout light felt over a dark background used in the making of the belt is exemplified on a magnificent scale in this beautiful hanging by Kopel Gurwin. Photographed at the Israeli Art Center.

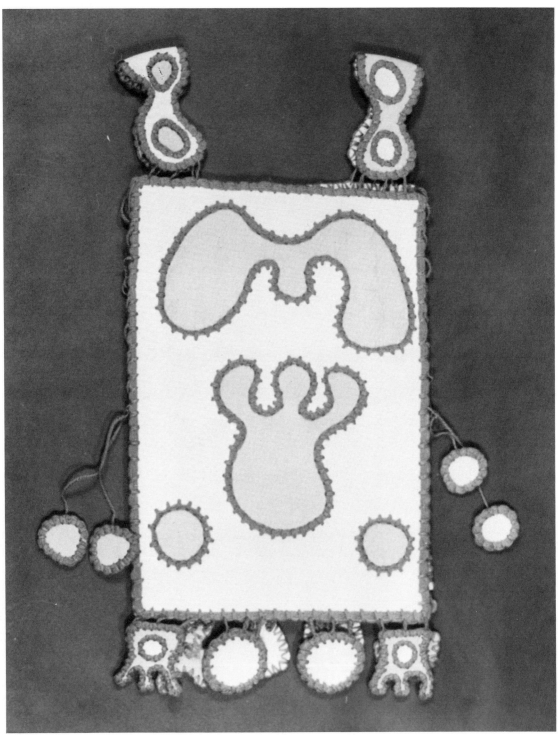

Bright orange and hot pink were used to fashion this striking pinafore. Simple bold shapes were cut out of the top, which was then embroidered to the back with couched yarn. The little dangles and shoulder straps are made in the same way. Marilyn Motz, artist.

APPLIQUÉD VESTS

When making a vest out of felt, just cut a double pattern, using one as a lining. Joan Schulze applied simple bold shapes and bits of lace to the front of her vest. The back is a whole garden of appliquéd leaves, trees, grass, and flowers.

Front view of Felt Garden vest by Joan Schulze.

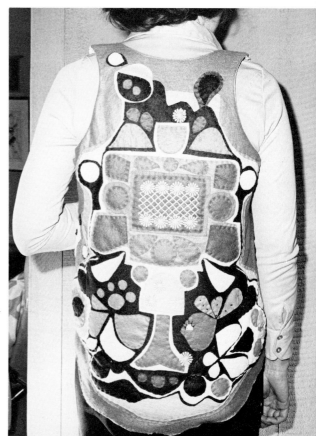

Felt Garden vest, rear view.

APPLIQUÉD SKIRTS

Shulamit Litan splashes a skirt of felt and cotton squares with simple appliqué designs. Photographed at the Israeli Art Center.

GAME RUGS

The popularity of backgammon and chess among a group of Albany State University students inspired a double-sided rug-hanging. Loops were used at either end of the rug instead of fringes, so that a stick could be pushed through one end for easy hanging.

Checkerboard side of game rug.

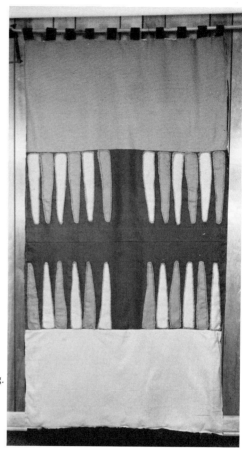

Backgammon side of game rug.

Design Inspirations for Appliqué

Traditional patchwork designs are much simpler to work out in felt than other materials and the many bold colors available help to create distinctly contemporary designs.

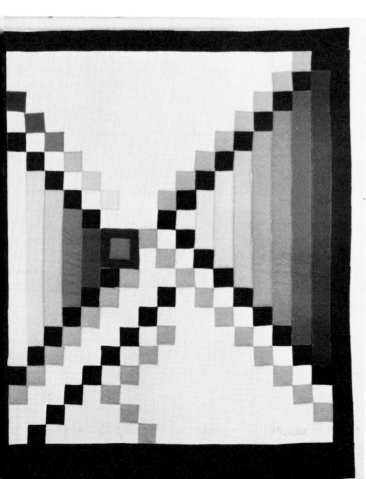

The traditional log cabin pattern is worked into a bold, modern pattern by Michiko Sato. (See color section.)

Lucette Rousseau gathered her inspiration for this mural-sized hanging from a trip to Yucatan. (See color section.)

Closeup detail of Lucette's hanging.

Kopel Gurwin's felt appliqués are sewn to linen and mounted on wood panels. Photographed at Israeli Art Center.

Hebrew letters serve as a focal point for another Kopel Gurwin hanging. Photographed at Israeli Art Center.

Upper left
These unusual sculptural forms began as prints. Arms are movable. Fran Willner.
Upper right
Appliquéd tapestry inspired by a trip to Yucatán. Lucette Rousseau.
Bottom left
"Windows." Felt quilt by Marta Del Fara. Courtesy artist.
Bottom right
Reverse appliqué collar necklace and patchwork yo-yos with mirrors and crochet edging. Elyse Sommer.

Stuffed and beaded hanging. Shulamit Litan. Photographed at Israeli Art Center.

Reverse appliqué and crochet vest. Elyse Sommer.

Cigar box recycled into a soft sculpture. Elyse Sommer.

Felt adds color and design value to wood construction by Ahuvah Bebe Dushey. Photo Kahane/-Kirshner, Image 1.

"Sea Fair," a 6' X 26' mural by Ray Ameijide. Photo courtesy Anchor Savings Bank, New York.

Felt appliquéd skirt by Shulamit Litan. Photographed at Israeli Art Center.

"Super Sam" by Paula Gollhardt. Courtesy artist.

"Catchall Landscape." Elyse Sommer.

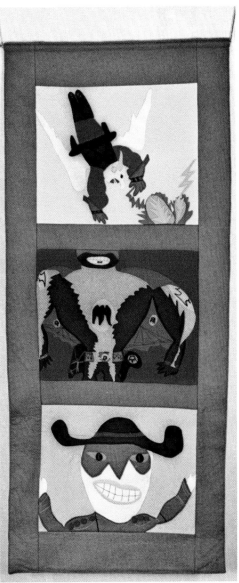

Mother-son collaboration: sketches by Kenzo Sato, aged 8, worked out in felt by mother Michiko.

Felt appliqué wall plaque before and after stitchery is added. Sharon Fields.

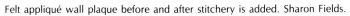

Michiko Sato interprets the Log Cabin motif in a distinctly modern hanging.

Handmade felt from the studio of Barbara Setsu Pickett. Courtesy artist.

"Rainbow Quest." Hanging combining felt, silk, and velvet. Caroline Wickham. Photo courtesy artist.

View of the studio where Australian artist Fay Bottrell creates her soft hard-edge felt paintings.

Felt, plus bits of fur, and fantasy combined into a trio of doll sophisticates by Sharon Fields.

Experiments in coiled strips of felt. Michiko Sato.

Kopel Gurwin's imposing felt banners are inspired by biblical themes. Photographed at Israeli Art Center.

Another figurative painting in felt on linen.

Translating a painting into felt appliqué offers an interesting challenge. Here is a work by Paul Klee adapted by an occupational therapy student of Renee Breskin Adams.

Young artists fortunate enough to have equally talented mothers might see their drawings brought to life via felt appliqués. To wit, Michiko Sato's translation of son Kenzo's heroes.

Original drawing by Kenzo (made when he was 8) with close-up of Michiko's interpretation.

Favorite stories are another inspirational theme for the appliqué artist. Here is one of a whole series of fairy tale appliqués by Eva Ludwig. Photo courtesy artist.

The basic themes of human relationships lend themselves to felt appliqué. Note the effective use of small pearl buttons against the black appliqué shapes. Michiko Sato.

Caroline Wickham's "Rainbows" was inspired by Pete Seeger's album "The Rainbow Quest." To make the hanging the artist worked in units measuring 15 X 24 inches, beginning each at one end of two rainbows and working out in strips which changed their directions. Felt was used predominantly for the rainbow colors, with some satin and velvet. The final assembly of the appliqué squares was done by means of linking each unit with bias tape.

Detail of "Rainbows."

"St. Augustine" is another song interpretation by Caroline Wickham, inspired by Bob Dylan's "I Dreamed I Saw St. Augustine." The banner combines felt with a variety of printed fabrics.

4

Layered, Fringed, Ruffled, and Coiled

The felt you use is the result of the process of layering carded fibers and pressing them together. If you take a piece of thick industrial felt and work away at the edges you will find them loosening to reveal various thin layers. This is the same process by which you peel away the picture surface from a heavy print or postcard, since paper, like felt, is made in layers. Conversely, the craft felt sold in most stores is very thin, which permits you to build up your own layers of varying colors. The layers can be stitched together for a variety of interesting effects.

LAYERED LANDSCAPE CATCHALL

Mountain ranges are fun and easy to interpret in felt. Different colors can be used to suggest different seasons. In the demonstration photos that follow, the landscapes are layered, with tops of the mountains left unsewn so that they serve as catchall pockets.

Sun and cloud shapes are cut out of a piece of sky blue felt which is then layered against pieces of yellow and white felt. Hanging loops are pinned in place so that as much sewing as possible can be done in a single stitch-through operation, so that the loops will not have to be sewn on later.

Three mountain ranges are cut in double layers. Since the tops of the mountains will be left open the extra felt will give strength. By cutting the bottom in a darker shade, a bit of contrast or "shadow" is added.

The three mountains are pinned together and . . .

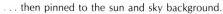

. . . then pinned to the sun and sky background.

By making your design longer, a more detailed landscape can be developed. The addition of embroidery adds detail and richness. A casing can be used instead of loops for hanging. (See color section.)

Here is the beginning of another landscape. The sun this time is not cut out but stitched, and a casing is made instead of hanging loops. Shown here is the sky layer with the highest mountain range in place.

A second scene, this time a house with grass and water are added.

A final mountain with grass and fern-stitched leaves completes the composition. (See color section.)

THE LAYERED LOOK INSPIRED BY HOUSE SHINGLES

When Joan Schulze saw a house in her neighborhood being shingled, she immediately thought of her huge basket of felt scraps. The result was an unusual felt-shingled planter. To make the planter waterproof, Joan cut clear plastic 1 inch higher than the pot to be covered and approximately two inches longer than the circumference of the pot. She then sewed the felt to the plastic. The lower end of the plastic was turned under and tacked down to form the finished planter. More felt-plus-plastic ideas from Joan in chapter 8.

Shingle planter cover. Joan Schulze.

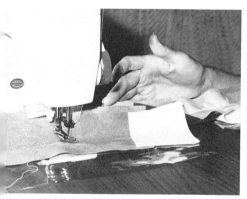

To make her planter cover Joan collected lots of felt scraps and overlapped her sorted pieces as she sewed. Plastic is added to the outside to waterproof the cover.

Michiko Sato uses the layering tech-nique to create a handsome hang-ing in shades of pink. The layered squares at the bottom of each side are sewn around a small piece of wood which acts as a weight.

Here Michiko uses the layering technique to create still another interpretation of the Log Cabin design she likes so much. She creates a unique look by leaving the top of each layer open to form a pocket. Green and purple are used in striking contrast against white.

Detail of Michiko Sato's layered Log Cabin hanging.

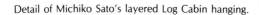

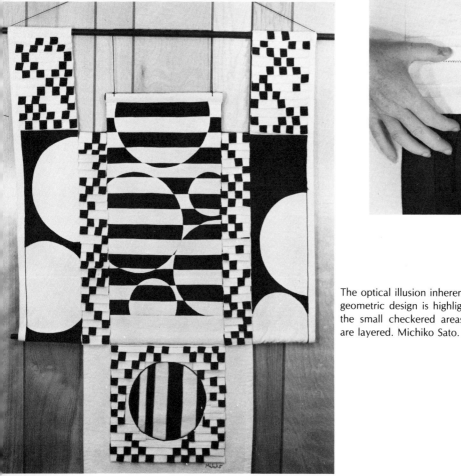

The optical illusion inherent in this geometric design is highlighted by the small checkered areas which are layered. Michiko Sato.

Fringed Felt

Felt is ideal for fringing since it won't unravel. Let's look at 2 fringed body ornaments to see how simply and handsomely felt fringing can be used.

FRINGED BEAD NECKLACE

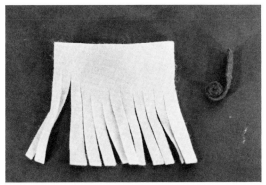

A piece of felt 3" wide X 4" long is fringed two-thirds of the way up. A small bead is made by coiling a strip of felt. (See more about coiling later.)

The tiny coiled bead is rolled into the larger fringed bead.

The felt beads are alternated with other beads to complete the necklace.

This complicated-looking body ornament by Marilyn Motz is really very simple to make.

A circle large enough for the head to slip through is cut out of a single piece of felt (18" X 36"). Fringes are cut all around. Couching and beads add the finishing touches.

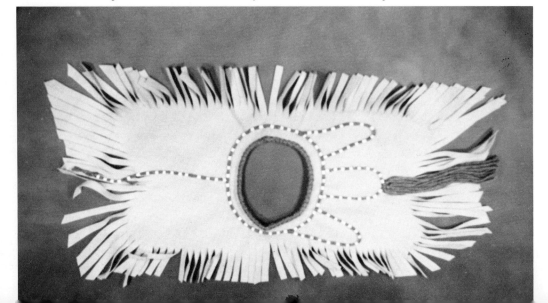

Felt Ruffles

Ruffles and coils lend themselves to a good deal of design experimentation. The ideas presented here can be expanded upon in an infinite variety of ways.

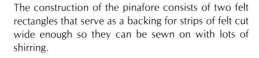

Felt ruffles add bouffant charm to this child's pinafore by Marilyn Motz.

The construction of the pinafore consists of two felt rectangles that serve as a backing for strips of felt cut wide enough so they can be sewn on with lots of shirring.

Detail of the ruffled pinafore.

Here is a somewhat more sophisticated project made with the same ruffling technique used for the child's pinafore. Evening bag in brilliant orange, pink, and yellow. Marilyn Motz.

FELT ROSETTES, OR YO-YOS

Yo-yos, or fabric rosettes, were a popular part of the patchwork scene of the 1920s. Basting stitches are made all around fabric circles and then gathered or ruffled together. Yo-yos made of felt require no seam edges and have a rich textural look. Mirrors or bits of fleece can be inserted into the felt circles before pulling the gathers tight. Necklaces, hangings, and vests are just some of the things to be made by linking yo-yos, or rosettes, together.

MIRROR ROSETTE NECKLACE

Basting stitches are made all around cut felt circle.

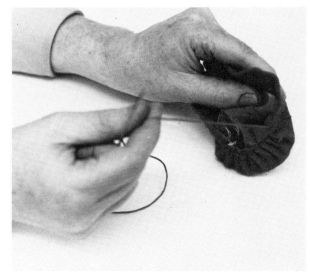

The stitches are gathered in—and a mirror is inserted before the final tightening of the ruffle.

Yo-yo Mirror Necklace.

A hanging of felt rosettes in varying sizes, with bits of fleece stuffed into the center to suggest flower center. The flower pot was holed with a hole puncher and sewn to a lighter beige felt pot.

Yo-yos, or rosettes, can also be assembled into handsome vests. Note the smaller rosettes used along the edges of this bolero.

Coiled Felt

Rolling strips of felt into beads requires patience, but the design possibilities are quite exciting and make this technique well worth trying. Michiko Sato, who has done a great deal of experimentation with this type of felt design, cuts all her strips by hand. We would recommend cutting the strips on a paper cutter as shown on page 21. This is not only a time-saver but makes for greater accuracy.

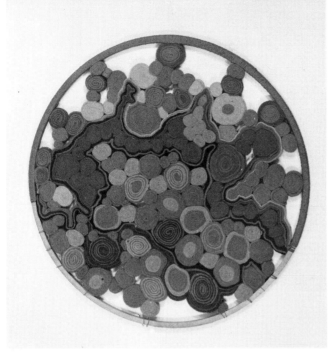

Michiko Sato varies her coils by using felt strips of different lengths and by combining different colors into one coil. She stitches her coils together but they could be secured with glue. Here lots and lots of coils are most effectively framed inside a partially wrapped wooden hoop. (See color section.)

Michiko assembles more coils into a hanging that can be suspended from the center of the ceiling as well as against the wall.

If you don't have the patience to make enough felt coils for a large piece, you might think of them as accents, like fringes, as in this beautiful appliquéd hanging. Michiko Sato.

Felt strips can be squashed and pressed into still different shapes. Michiko Sato aptly named this experiment "Fig Newtons." (See color section.)

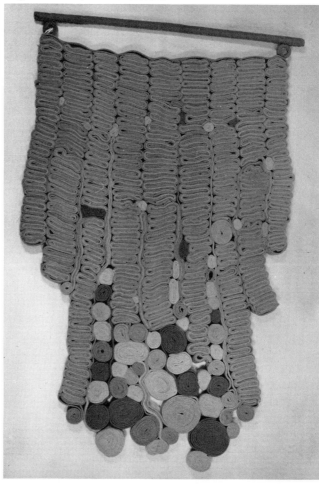

5

Stuffed Forms

Stuffing is the felt artist's sculpturing material. Whether you work a bit of polyester fiber into an appliqué hanging or use the stuffing more freely to turn the appliqué into an independent sculptural form, the extra softness and roundness of stuffing adds that "please touch me" quality to your creations. From a utilitarian standpoint, stuffing adds warmth as well as texture. Polyester fiber, Dacron batting, cut-up hose, bits of wool saved from stitchery work, shredded foam—the choice of stuffing materials is largely a matter of preference and availability.

From Appliqué to Sculpture

In chapter 3 a bag decorated with two appliquéd figures was shown. By cutting the appliqué out in duplicate, sewing the two shapes together, and stuffing before sewing closed completely, the figures become independent sculptures. It is a good idea to cut the shapes slightly larger than you would for an appliqué to allow for the displacement resulting from the stuffing.

67

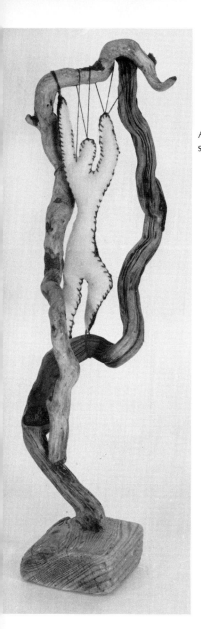

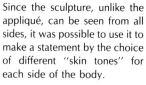

An appliqué which became a sculpture.

Since the sculpture, unlike the appliqué, can be seen from all sides, it was possible to use it to make a statement by the choice of different "skin tones" for each side of the body.

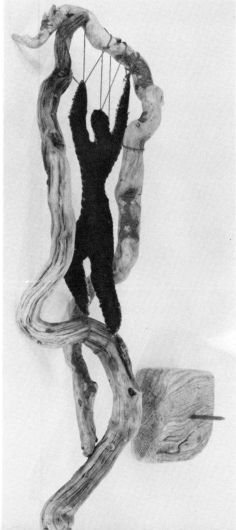

The driftwood frame was nailed together from two curved branches. A nail was drilled through the stands, with the point going through from the underside through the top. A hole, large enough to accommodate the nail, was drilled into the bottom of the frame. Thus, the frame can be slipped over the nail. It is not permanently secured so that it can swivel around on the base stand.

Beaded and Stuffed

Stuffing gives small felt pieces sufficient firmness and body to make them wearable. Beads, in colors to highlight or echo the fabric shade, add elegance and texture to the surface.

Small beads and appliqués raised up by stuffing add tactile strength and excitement to this stunning hanging by Shulamit Litan. Photographed at Israeli Art Center. (See color section.)

Stuffing and antique beads give body and elegance to Ahuvah Bebe Dushey's wine-colored pendant. Photo Kahan/Kirshner, Image 1.

AHUVAH BEBE DUSHEY

Shades of lavender are stuffed, encrusted with antique beads, and mounted on a block of granite. "Entity" by Ahuvah Bebe Dushey. Photo Kahan/Kirshner, Image 1.

Quilts

Marta dal Farra designs her 4-layered, Dacron-stuffed quilts around themes ranging from the theatrical to nature. She makes her backing from two layers of felt with Dacron batting sewn in between as for a pillow. The appliquéd squares are made separately and stitched through the felt-Dacron-felt backing which makes the squares puff out for an extrafull effect. (See color section.)

Quilted Water Hanging, 35" X 50". Marta dal Farra. John Evans photographer.

"All the World's a Stage", 65" X 41". Marta dal Farra.

The following sketches show the steps by which Marta assembles her
quilts:

Marta's quilts start with four layers of muslin-felt-felt-muslin
stitched together on three sides,
like a pillow.

Dacron batting is hand-sewn to
the top muslin layer.

The "pillow" is turned inside
out so that the felt layers are on
top, as shown in the sketch, and
the open side is stitched closed.

The appliquéd squares are
made separately and stitched
through the entire backing,
which makes the squares puff
out for a rich, full effect. (See
color section.)

WEARABLE QUILTS

This quilted chest warmer is made by cutting the chest square and the neckband out of one piece of felt (use a double layer for extra warmth—and Dacron batting between these layers for *still* more warmth). Felt squares in contrasting colors are appliquéd and then attached to the background by sewing down three sides only. These little appliqué pockets are then stuffed with leftover wool yarns and tops stitched closed.

The quilted chestwarmer can be worn by young or old, male or female.

Dolls

Of course there's nothing that invites touching more than a doll, and
no book on felt would be complete without including this very universal
type of sculpture.

A simple, totally huggable shape is felt appliquéd and fringed by
Michiko Sato. The reversed side features another doll design.

PILLOW DOLLS

Even those who feel they have "outgrown" dolls (if doll collectors
and artists making dolls are any indication, no one ever outgrows dolls!)
can indulge their fantasies for something bright, gay, and whimsical with
pillow dolls.

Jean Ray Laury uses a plain pillow square as the base of a happy little fellow with appliquéd felt features, fringed hair, and bits of lace and ribbon. Photo Gayle Smalley. From *Doll Making: A Creative Approach* by Jean R. Laury, c. 1970 by Litton Educational Publishing, Inc.

Sharon Fields combines calico with felt. The cat's head is a separate little stuffed pillow sewn to the stuffed body. The tail is also made and attached separately.

Triangular shapes lend themselves to lots of whimsical pillow-doll forms. The separate legs are jointed by stitching across the knees. Felt is used mostly as an accent here, for face, features, hair, and arms. Sharon Fields, artist.

Here's a trio from Sharon Fields's gallery of glamorous people. Felt is contrasted with fur, satin, and beads. The bodies are cut in two solid pieces, with details sewn on. Legs are jointed for easy sitting. (See color section.)

CARICATURE DOLLS

Paula Gollhardt's dolls are all based on puns: Midnite Sheriff, Star Piece, Elly Fant are all cut from two pieces, stuffed, and stitched together.

Lavender felt with lavender lace and a "diamond" neckband make this quite unmistakably "The Mother of the Bride." The heart-shaped arms are made from two separately stuffed pieces. Paula Gollhardt.

"Howee" evolved from a simple basic shape. The Indian's feather is stiffened with bits of wire.

"Udder Nonsense" by Paula Gollhardt.

Stuffed Chess Set

Chess sets have fascinated sculptors through the ages. Wood, clay, metal, plastic, are just some of the media used. We used black and white felt to make a whimsical sort of chess set. The owl pieces range from three to four inches in height. Anyone not wishing to make a complete set could use individual pieces as ornaments.

The six basic chess pieces: *top left:* castle, king; *bottom left:* queen, knight; *right:* bishop, pawn. The opposing side has black bodies with white trims.

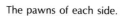
The pawns of each side.

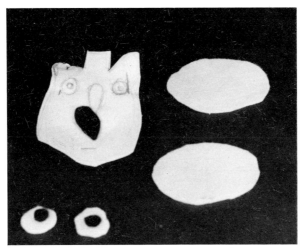

The basic pieces were cut to match a roughly sketched paper pattern. Protrusions like the castle square between this owl castle's ears are cut as part of the main piece. The circle is for the standing base. The pieces could be weighted with some pebbles, but the stuffing will make them self-supporting without extra weights.

The wings of the king, queen, and bishop are differentiated for easy identification by players. The bishop's wings are fringed and sewn from back to front, like a cape. The queen's wings are inlaid in contrast color and stitched down at the side. The king's wings are tacked down at the front, but allowed to flap.

6

Glued and Stitched

For those who do not like sewing, felt's easy compatibility with glue opens up many avenues for creative exploration. Whether your glued felt projects are small like the puzzles which follow, or mural-sized like Ray Ameijide's magnificent "Sea Fair," remember to avoid saturating your material with glue. Instead, apply the glue to the surface to be covered, rather than directly to the material. We've found white glues such as Sobo or Elmer's Glue-All suitable. One artist told us she uses household cement to avoid having to wait for the glue to set. If you plan anything large, we suggest you experiment with a variety of glues, glues diluted with water, and glue used full strength.

Felt Jigsaw Puzzles

Felt jigsaw puzzles are good gift items, beginning experiments for young children, or occupational therapy for hospital patients. The idea for these puzzles was first suggested to us by Bucky King.

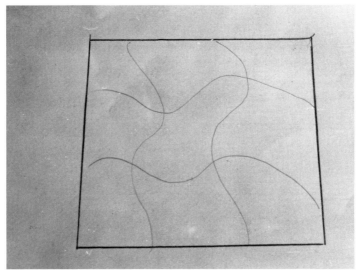

Draw two vertical and two horizontal lines on a cardboard square. Use pencil
very lightly.

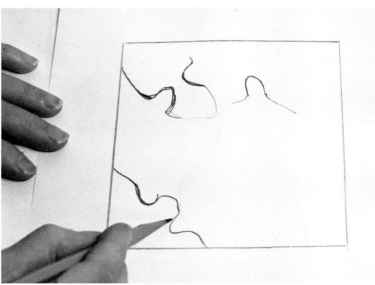

Erase portions of the lines and add puzzle bumps at random.

Cut out each piece of the cardboard pattern; then glue felt to each side of the cardboard pieces.

Individual puzzle pieces can be used as the basis of an attractive novelty necklace. Use an embroidery needle to pierce through the felt-covered cardboard. Insert a jump ring through each hole and then thread a neckband through the jump rings. The illustrated necklace has a crochet chain neckband. You could use braided wool, ribbons, or a regular jewelry chain.

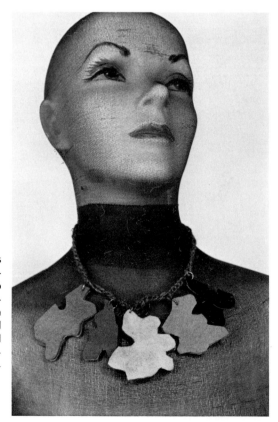

Felt Tanagrams

The old Chinese tanagram puzzles were usually made from black paper since the idea behind the puzzles was to figure out how the 7 basic pieces which make up the tanagram were used to form the silhouette shape. (In America tanagrams were known as silhouettes). By gluing pieces of felt to cut cardboard the puzzles gain a nice tactile quality and can be worked in reverse: The player tries to combine the pieces to create shapes of his own invention. A double set of basic pieces literally doubles the possibilities. A particularly pleasing silhouette or set of silhouettes might be mounted and used as a plaque or hanging.

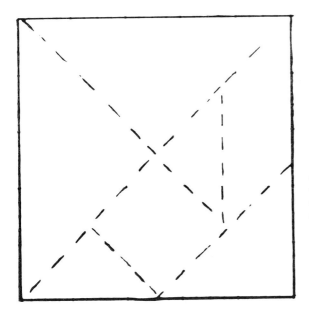

Divide a 5" square into seven parts as shown in the diagram. Cut out each part and glue felt to each side of the cutout shapes. The shapes can be reassembled into the original square. Or . . .

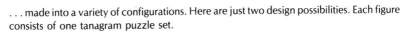

. . . made into a variety of configurations. Here are just two design possibilities. Each figure consists of one tanagram puzzle set.

Glued and Stitched Boxes

A variety of box shapes can be created from ordinary shirt cardboard, with felt used as a lining and covering fabric. We've used some stitching in combination with the gluing.

GLUED AND STITCHED LETTER BOX

A large cardboard rectangle, with corners cut off so the sides will meet when folded up, is covered on both sides with felt. White glue diluted by 1/3 with water was used. The fabric was carefully pressed against the glue-covered cardboard and smoothed out to prevent wrinkles.

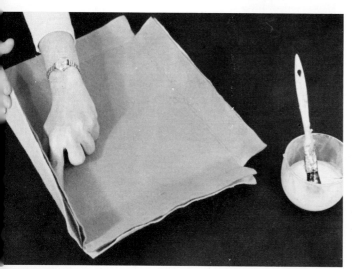

The sides should be bent up immediately so that a smooth folding line can be made.

The corners are overstitched with embroidery yarn. For a finished edge, you can overstitch all around the top of the box.

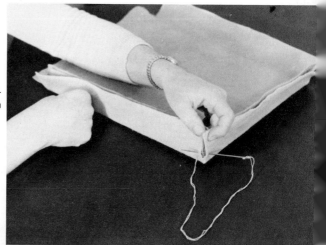

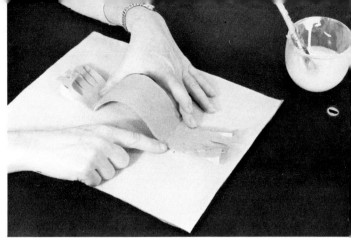

The lid of the box is made the same size as the bottom, without the sides. A strip of cardboard is covered with felt, cut about 3 inches longer than the cardboard at each end. The ends are fringed, and the handle is bent and glued to the top of the lid.

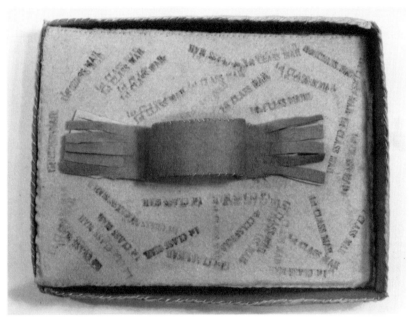

The finished box is decorated with stamping done with an ordinary mailing stamper.

HEXAGONAL BOX

Boxes need not be square or rectangular only, but can be round, oval, hexagonal, or octagonal. The technique is the same as for the letter box, except for the lid. It is cut to match the bottom, though it is somewhat larger.

Draw your basic shape accurately onto cardboard and cut out.

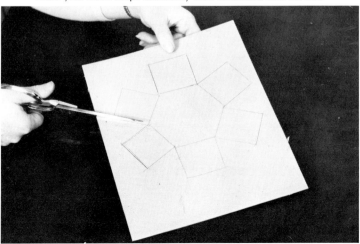

Cut felt to match the box and glue first to the outside and then the inside of the box.

The box top is cut ½" larger all around but with shorter sides.

The bright green and yellow of the finished box are muted with an overlay of lace salvaged from a flea market.

A Felt Mural

Ray Ameijide is a paper sculptor who turned to felt for its added color and texture. His 26' X 6' "Sea Fair" is on permanent display at the Anchor Savings Bank in New York. Ten historical nautical figures, from Leif Ericsson to Robert Fulton, are represented against a background of ten fully constructed corresponding vessels. The central motif is highlighted by the artist's personal interpretation of mythical elements. The work encompasses over ten thousand individual pieces of felt and supportive materials (the felt is glued onto white cardboard) and took over five months to complete.

When doing felt sculpture of this type, even the basic sketches must be done with the finished three-dimensional forms in mind. Many components of the finished work are not seen which is why the artist compares his mural to an iceberg.

"Sea Fair," Ray Ameijide. Photo courtesy Anchor Savings Bank. (See color section.)

Close-up of one of the vessels.

Close-up of one of the seafarers.

Another close-up.

Felt and Crochet

Crochet can add a distinctive finishing touch to felt designs. A sweater or vest will be completed much faster when large areas are made in felt. The crocheted portions add easy-fitting stretchability to a garment. Crocheters who have enjoyed combining crochet with leather will find felt is more colorful and less expensive than leather.

Stitches can be worked off any felt piece simply by edging the felt with blanket stitches and then single crocheting into the loops of the blanket stitches. The projects illustrated in this chapter employ mostly basic crochet stitches.

Yo-Yos and Crochet

A good way to illustrate the accent value of crochet is to go back to one of our earlier projects, the yo-yo mirror necklace in chapter 4.

In case you don't know how to crochet, study the following photographs to see how the single crochet is done.

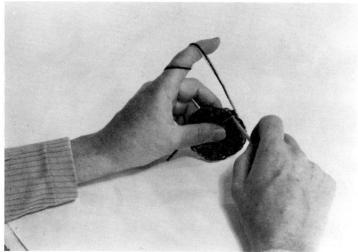

Insert your hook into the loop of the blanket stitch.

Bring your yarn over in front of the two loops and pull through one loop.

Yarn over and pull through the two remaining loops. Your single crochet is now complete.

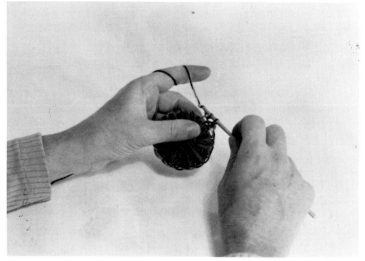

Here is the yo-yo necklace seen earlier in the book, but with the addition of crocheting. The little bumps are picots which are made by chaining up for 3 stitches and then crocheting into the same space as the chain.

Another variation achieved with the combination of yo-yos and crochet. Small African beads are stitched to the center of each yo-yo. A small yo-yo is used as a button to close the neckband, which gains interest with an additional row of stitches worked onto the top of the neckband.

Crochet Lends Importance to Small Felt Pieces

By adding crochet all around the small reverse appliqué sample illustrated in chapter 3, the sample grew into a large piece that doubles as a hanging and body ornament.

Here is the hanging with the top and side bands tied around the body to create an unusual body adornment.

REVERSE APPLIQUÉ AND CROCHET VEST

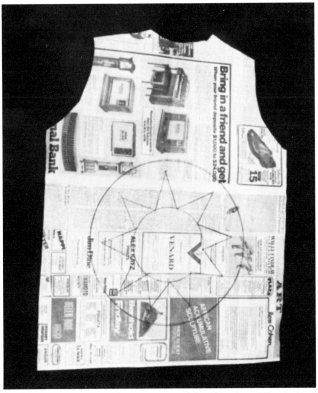

A vest pattern is cut out of newspaper and the central motif for the back of the vest is drawn onto the pattern.

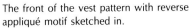
The front of the vest pattern with reverse appliqué motif sketched in.

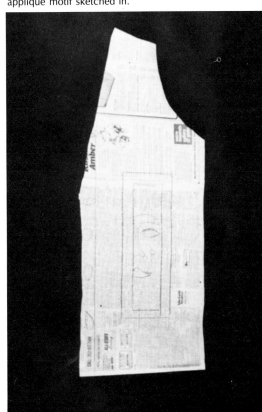

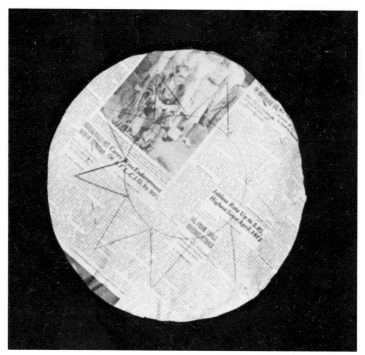

The design portion is cut out of the pattern and pinned to a layer of felt cut to match.

The portion of the sun with the spoked edges is cut out of the top layer (be sure to save your cutaway), and the cut layer is pinned to a second felt circle. The second circle is marked off with the features which will be cut out. After this the two circles will be sewn to a third, back-up circle.

Here is the completed appliqué design with crochet worked off from the central circle. (See color section.)

Front view of the vest. The buttons are handmade from some old Mah-Jongg tiles, sliced and sanded with a power tool.

This necklace was made from the portion cut away from the first layer of the vest's central design. The necklace was in turn worked into a three-layered reverse appliqué design, embellished with beads. (See color section.)

BOX SCULPTURE WITH FELT AND CROCHET

A cigar box can be covered with felt that is stuffed with polyester stuffing to soften the hardness of the basic box. The concept of hard-into-soft invites imaginative experimentation.

The sides of the box are covered first. Stuffing is worked into the felt covering, which is attached with a staple gun.

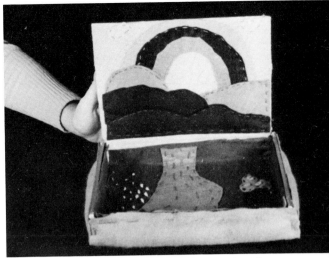

The inside of the box is lined with two appliquéd landscapes which, once stitched, are attached to the box with glue.

For the top of the box a tree is cut from two pieces of brown felt, stuffed and trimmed with green mohair crochet leaves (picot stitches). The tree is sewn to a grass green felt base that is decorated with flowers made by crocheting small circles and ruffling them by rapidly increasing all around, three or four times in a stitch. Some of the tiniest flowers are embroidered French knots.

Stuffing is worked under the top covering material, which is then stapled in place.

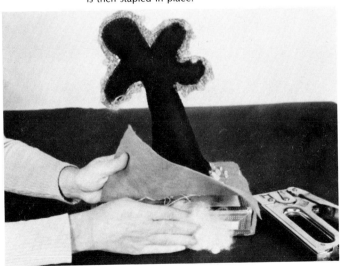

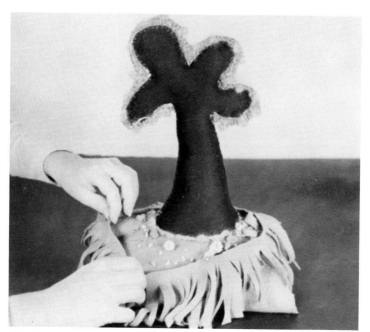

An open rectangle with fringed edges is put around the garden and sewn in place. (See color section.)

8

A Miscellany of
Felt Ideas

Felt and the Printmaker

You can print on felt with an ordinary mailing stamp as shown in the handmade letter box in chapter 6 or use other printing techniques such as block printing or silk-screening. Fran Willner, a very talented and innovative graphics designer, has translated a number of her prints into truly distinctive felt works.

Here, at the top, we see Fran Willner's original print on felt. In the middle the print takes
on sculptural dimension with the addition of machine quilting worked against a ½" foam
backing. At the bottom "Reclining Woman" is completed with added embroidery details
and a crocheted border. Photo courtesy artist.

Dollmakers might borrow Fran's technique of printing on felt, then cutting out her shapes in duplicate and stuffing and stitching them into "Felt People." (See color section.) Pushpins make the arms and legs movable. Photo courtesy artist.

Fran often uses the same basic print to create a variety of effects. For example, here is one of her felt people encased in Plexiglas. "Earth Mother" is a free-standing sculpture. Photo courtesy artist.

Here's another Willner print translated into a pillow doll with bits of lace, jewelry, and stitchery added on. Photo courtesy New Jersey Newsphotos.

Another unusual sofa pillow emerges from a print. The felt face is zippered into a felt sleeping bag, which is lined with tie-dyed cotton. In this photo we also see the print on paper. Courtesy New Jersey Newsphotos.

Felt Encased in Soft Plastic

Since felt, unlike some fabrics, does not lend itself to frequent washing, one way of giving it total utility is to encase it in the clear plastic fabric that is sold in most hardware stores. The plastic adds a glitter and brightness and gloss that appeals to many modern artists. It can be stitched by hand or machine. Place mats, baby bibs, small screens, tree ornaments, boxes, and baby blocks are just some of the types of felt projects that are particularly suited to the felt and plastic combination.

Plastic-covered felt planter with some needlepoint canvas and appliqué added. Joan Schulze.

A 4-panel table screen, encased in plastic. Joan Schulze.

Felt and Silk

While plastic is primarily a practical addition to felt, the same principle
of sandwiching felt underneath a clear fabric works to mute and enrich
the felt if silk instead of plastic is used. To illustrate this Joan Schulze
designed a truly elegant blouse.

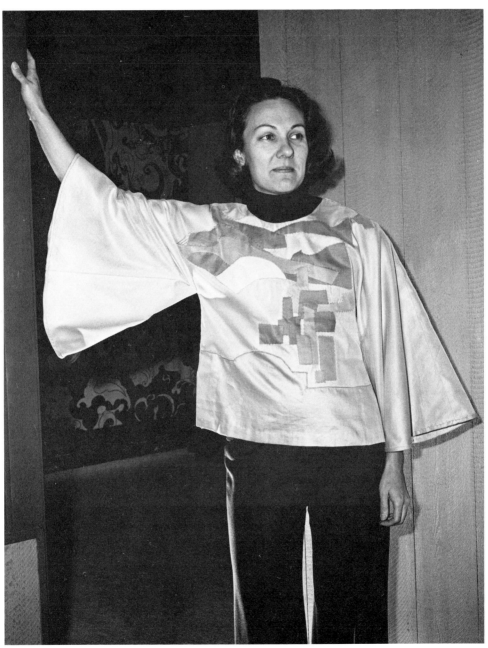

The basic pattern is cut from cotton. Felt is appliquéd to the cotton underlayer for design
and an overlay of silk organza completes the look.

Crayon-Batiked Felt

Felt was crayon-batiked, then appliquéd to felt sides of a box. The box was put together in sections with some machine embroidery for more emphasis. The final construction was done with hand sewing.

Wood Constructions with Felt

Since Ahuvah Bebe Dushey's constructions are born from materials that would seem unlikely art objects to most people, she likes to add lots of other unexpected touches. In the following pictures we see her experiments in marrying bright bits of felt with a variety of natural and man-made discards. All photos by Kirshner/Kahane, Image 1.

"For Whom the Bell Tolls." Antique wood with felt.

"Transcendence." Antique wood construction with felt.

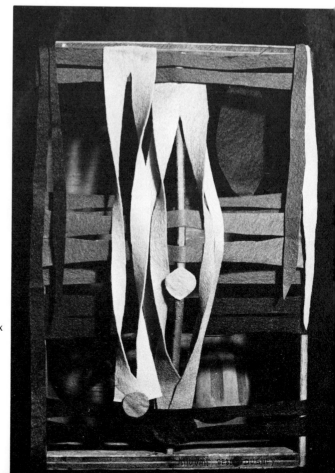

"Interactions." Antique toolbox with stretched felt strips.

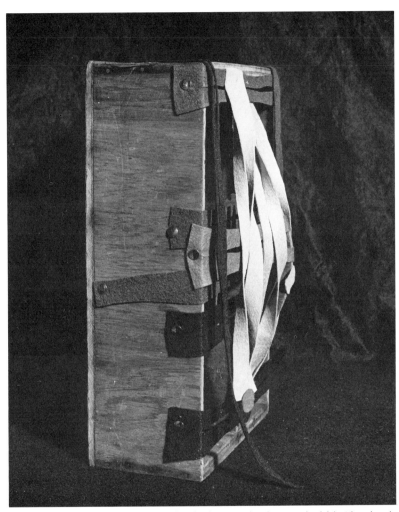

Sideview of "Interactions" revealing the shadow cast by the stretched felt. Thumbtacks were used to attach the felt. These could be bought in colors to match or contrast with the fabric.

Michiko Sato uses wood largely as hanging dowels for her appliquéd hangings. Since she always paints the dowels to match the main felt color or to contrast with it, she decided to experiment by integrating some of her dowels into the design. This striking hanging in red, green, and yellow with black dowels proved the success of her attempt.

Yarn-Framed Patches

Marilyn Motz loves the contrast of thick yarns against felt. She likes to use small patches of felt, with the yarn worked around the edge to create a richly textured frame. She uses wrapping or close-together overcast stitches to create these framed edges and sometimes adds couching to build a color pattern.

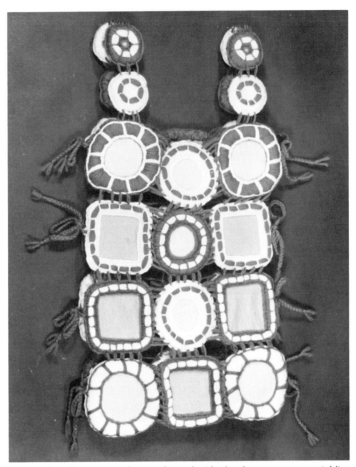

Hot pink and orange patches are framed with closely overcast yarn. Additional threads of contrasting yarn are couched in between some of the overcasting.

Each of the wrapped patches appliquéd to this stunning black felt bag is made from a base of two felt circles cut like doughnuts. A piece of cardboard is sandwiched between the two felt circles to give body to the patch. Black and white yarn is wrapped around the base to form a geometric pattern. Couching adds variety to the patterns.

Both the front and the back of the bag are appliquéd with the wrapped patches, each of which could be used as a pendant, belt buckle, or start of a variety of body ornaments.

Felt Tubes

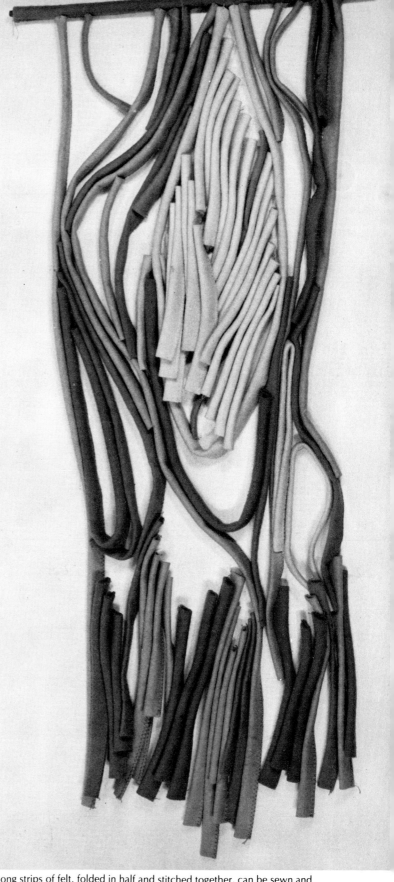

Long strips of felt, folded in half and stitched together, can be sewn and twisted into interesting tubular shapes. The tubes in this hanging by Michiko Sato are unstuffed.

If felt strips are worked around wire, upholstery cord, or clothesline cord, very solid tubes result. Madge Copeland applied this principle to a felt basket. She sewed long strips of felt around a clothesline core making her seam as close to the cord as possible. (She used the zipper foot on her sewing machine.) Several colors of felt were worked onto a 4-yard length of clothesline. She then used needle and thread invisibly to coil the basket.

Close-up of Madge's felt basketry coils.

Bibliography

Coats and Clark Book #50. *100 Embroidery Stitches*. New York: Coats and Clark Company, 1973.

EMERY, IRENE. *The Primary Structure of Fabrics*. Washington, D.C.: Textile Museum, 1966. "Felt," *Ciba Review* #29, November 1958. "Felted and Knotted Fabrics in Turkestan." *Ciba Review* #40, August 1941.

HESS, KATHARINE PADDOCK. *Textile Fibers and Their Use*. 5th ed., Philadelphia: J. B. Lippincott Co., 1954.

LAUFER, BERTHOLD. *Early History of Felt*. Chicago: Western Felt Works, 1930.

LAURY, JEAN RAY. *Doll Making: A Creative Approach*. New York: Litton Educational Publishing Co., 1970.

PATERA, CHARLOTTE. *The Appliqué Book*. Des Moines, Iowa: Meredith Corporation, 1974.

PETERSON, GRETTA, and SVENNAS, ELSE. *Handbook of Stitches*. New York: Van Nostrand-Reinhold, 1946, 1966.

SOMMER, ELYSE. *A New Look at Crochet*. New York: Crown, 1975.

———. *A Patchwork, Appliqué and Quilting Primer*. New York: Lothrop, Lee and Shepard, 1975.

VON BERGEN, WERNER, and MAUERSBERGER, HERBERT R. *American Wool Handbook*. New York: Textile Book Publishers, Inc., 1948.

Sources of Supplies

The materials used to make the items illustrated throughout this book are readily available in most stores carrying fabrics and needlecraft supplies. Some stores may not carry a complete line of felt colors or felts in different grades. Those who would like to experiment with feltmaking may not be able to obtain raw fleece in their neighborhood yarn shop. Following are some mail order sources for felt, fleece, yarns, beads, and stuffing. The listing is by no means complete or given to indicate our endorsement of any products. For ongoing information about sources of supplies as well as news about fabric and fiber happenings in general, the reader is referred to a group of special interest magazines.

Dick Blick
P. O. Box 1268
Galesburg, Ill. 61401
Felt, yarns, beads, paper cutters. Large catalogue

Carmel Valley Weavers Supply
Box 77 A Route K
Del Mar, Calif. 92014
Fleece, yarns, beads. Samples, 50¢

116

Colorbelle Ltd.
2104 Dufferin St.
Toronto, 345, Ontario, Canada
Felt in wide variety of colors

Commonwealth Felt Co.
211 Congress Street
Boston, Mass. 02110
Felt in all grades and colors

Coulter Studios
118 E. 59 Street
New York, N.Y. 10022
Imported yarns and fleeces. Send stamped, addressed envelope for
samples

Dharma Trading Co.
P. O. Box 1288
Berkeley, Calif. 94701
Fleece, yarns. Catalogue: 50¢

DKDesign
P. O. Box 7527
Oakland, Calif. 94601
Odd-sized Dacron batting at some discount. Send stamped, addressed
envelope for price list

Economy Handicrafts
4711 Francis Lewis Blvd.
Flushing, N.Y. 11363
General crafts supplies, felt, yarns

Greentree Ranch Wools
163 N. Carter Lake Rd.
Loveland, Colo. 80537
Fleece, yarns. Inquire if their mixed dyed fleece sampler is available

Sachiye Jones
2050 Friendly
Eugene, Ore. 97405
Fleece, yarns

Lamb's End
16861 Hamilton Ave.
Highland Park, Mich. 48203
Fleece, yarns. Catalogue: $2.50, deductible from first order

Sears, Roebuck Co. (See phone book for store nearest you.)
Dacron batting and sewing supplies

Stearns & Foster, Quilting Department
Cincinnati, Ohio 45217
Batting for quilting

Special Interest Magazines

Artisan Crafts
Route 4, Box 179
Reeds Spring, Mo. 65737
Quarterly magazine for craftsmen

Crafts Horizon
44 W. 53rd St.
New York, N.Y. 10019
Bimonthly publication of American Crafts Council

Creative Crafts
Drawer 700
Newton, N.J. 07060
Bimonthly for amateur and professional hobbyists

Index